It's Not Your Fault, KoKo Bear

A Read-Together Book for Parents & Young Children During Divorce

Illustrated by Jane Prince

Vicki Lansky

author of *Vicki Lansky's* DIVORCE BOOK FOR PARENTS
Helping Your Children Cope With Divorce and Its Aftermath

BOOK PEDDLERS
MINNETONKA, MINNESOTA
Book trade distribution by Publishers Group West

Special thanks to:
Constance Ahrons, PhD; Gail Berkove, PhD; Melinda Blau; Sally Brush; Cynthia
 and Brittany Crosby; Miriam Galper Cohen; Elizabeth Hickey; Steve King, MSW;
Adaire Lassonde, SSND, LISW; Gary Neuman, PhD; Francie Paper; Dessa Rosman;
Pamela Panasiti Stettner; Meg Zweiback.

Illustrator: Jane Prince and her technical advisor Sam Murphy, age 11
Layout and design: MacLean & Tuminelly

ISBN 0-916-773-47-7 paperback
(ISBN 0-916773-46-9 hardcover)

———————————————————————————

Publisher's Cataloging-in-Publication
(Provided by Quality Books, Inc.)
Lansky, Vicki.
    It's not your fault, Koko Bear : a read-together book for
parents & young children during divorce / by Vicki Lansky ;
illustrated by Jane Prince. -- 1st ed.
    p. cm.
    SUMMARY: Koko Bear learns what divorce means, how to deal with
changes, how to recognize and deal with feelings, and that divorce
is not Koko's fault. Each page includes tips for parents.
    ISBN: 0-916773-47-7 (trade paper)
    ISBN: 0-916773-46-9 (cloth)

1. Divorce--Psychological aspects--Juvenile literature. 2.
Children of divorced parents--Psychology--juvenile literature.
I. Title

HQ772.5.L36 1998   [E]
                             QBI97-1307

———————————————————————————

*This book is available to divorce parent education groups, family therapists,
mediators and lawyers to help parents work through divorce. For a discount
when ordering 9 or more copies, contact the publisher at 1-800-255-3379.*

BOOK PEDDLERS
15245 Minnetonka Blvd, Minnetonka, MN 55345
612•912•0036   fax 612•912•0105

Printed in Hong Kong by Pettit Network Inc

99 00   01 02   10 9 8 7 6 5 4 3 2

Introduction for Parents

When children whose parents are divorcing realize that Mom or Dad has left the family home, their certainty that the other parent will not disappear is shaken. They often receive conflicting messages from their divorcing parents, adding to their confusion and anxiety. Children can make false assumptions—including self-blame—to try to deal with the insecure and changing world in which they now find themselves.

As children watch how their parents act out anger toward each other in the divorce process, how do they know that their parents won't act in a similar way toward them? Some children react by being very good, fearing that the same anger will be directed towards them—or, worse yet, that they will cause the other parent to leave, as well.

It is natural to be angry at an exiting spouse; it is not okay to show your anger in front of your children. You don't have to like your former (or soon-to-be-former) spouse to behave in a courteous manner. This is done every day by thousands of teeth-gritting adults. My book, *Vicki Lansky's Divorce Book for Parents*, can help you with the nuts and bolts of how to do this. The reward for such mature behavior is the emotional well-being of your children.

As you read *It's Not Your Fault, KoKo Bear*, you may think MaMa and PaPa Bear are unrealistically polite and even-tempered. KoKo's family might not look like your family. But it can, if you so choose. How you handle your parenting when you are parenting apart will make all the difference in the life of your child.

I hope that you will encourage your child to take this little book along to be read at each parent's home. Hearing the same message read by both Mom and Dad can reassure your child that he or she is loved and will be cared for by both of you.

— *Vicki Lansky*

One day MaMa and PaPa Bear say to KoKo, "We have something very difficult to tell you. We are getting a divorce, KoKo Bear."

KoKo Bear does not understand. "What is a divorce?" asks KoKo.

"Divorce is when grown-ups decide they will not live together anymore," answers MaMa Bear, "and one of them moves out of the house. Divorce means that now you will have two homes instead of one. PaPa and I each will have a home of our own and you will spend time in both of them. We both will still take care of you, but MaMa and PaPa Bear will live apart."

PaPa Bear tells KoKo, "I will be moving into a new place soon and it will be your home when you are with me."

KoKo is not happy. KoKo does not think this is good news.

- Children need to know what is happening and how they will be affected by your separation. This includes specific details about the time they will be spending with those they love—both of you, their grandparents, babysitters or even a pet.

- Children should never be asked who they want to live with or to take sides in one parent's anger toward the other. This presents a loyalty dilemma that can only confuse and upset them.

- Children think in simple and magical ways, believing that a mere wish or thought can come true. It is very easy for young children to believe that the divorce is their fault and that they can stop it by wishing hard enough.

- Children need to hear age-appropriate reasons for your divorce. They do not need to hear about your anger or your blame.

When PaPa Bear moves out of the house, everyone feels very sad. KoKo begins to cry.

"It's okay to cry, KoKo," says MaMa Bear. "Tears can help wash away some of the sad feelings. The divorce makes me sad, too, and there are times when I cry. I know sometimes PaPa Bear cries about the divorce, too."

KoKo says, "I want PaPa Bear to live here. I don't want him to leave. I don't want two homes!"

"I know it will be difficult not having PaPa live here," says MaMa Bear. "He won't be moving back, but PaPa will come here tomorrow to pick you up and take you to see his new home. Now let's pack some of your toys and clothes for you to take with you to PaPa's place."

KoKo is confused and scared.

- There is nothing more difficult than being separated from one you love. It's natural for a child to miss the other parent—even a parent who may seldom have been around. This does not mean that your child loves you any less.

- Crying is not a sign of weakness for a child—or a parent. Leaving or being left by someone you love hurts and crying is an honest and natural reaction to feeling sad.

- It's hard to accept children's hurt and anger over your divorce. Be patient. Dealing with separation is usually a much newer idea for them than it is for you.

- It is normal for children to hope their parents will reconcile, especially when their parents' anger isn't noisy or visible. Accepting your child's hopes and responding to their questions in a straight forward but kind manner is the best you can do.

'What do you think of my new home, KoKo?" asks PaPa Bear.

"It's okay, but it feels strange. Why do you have to live here, PaPa? I want all of us to live together. Did I do something bad? Is that why you left?" asks KoKo.

"Oh no, KoKo, you did not do anything wrong," answers PaPa Bear. "The divorce is not your fault. I didn't want to leave you. There are lots of hard-to-understand reasons why parents get a divorce. Grown-up bears can become very gruff and growly toward each other. They can hurt each other or change in ways that makes it impossible for them to live together.

"I am going to miss tucking you in when you are not here with me but I'll tuck you in nice and cozy when you are, KoKo. And we can talk on the phone every day. In fact, would you like to call MaMa Bear and say good night to her before I tuck you in and we read the story of *Goldilocks and the Three Chairs*?" asks PaPa Bear.

- It is not unusual for young children to be afraid to sleep in a new place, even if the parent or caregiver there is familiar and trusted.

- Encourage children's phone calls to the other parent but don't use these times as an opportunity to discuss highly-charged issues. Calls to grandparents on both sides can be a good investment in the future. Keeping a connection with extended families often helps children cope better.

- It is important to tell a child that you love and care about him or her and to make sure that your actions follow your words.

- Be prepared for various forms of the question "why?" Simply acknowledging your children's sadness, anger, frustration or whatever they feel can go a long way towards helping them accept the many changes in their lives.

MaMa and PaPa's divorce is making KoKo have many different kinds of feelings.

How do you think KoKo feels?

Should KoKo talk about these feelings?

What should MaMa and PaPa Bear say to KoKo?

Do you ever have feelings like KoKo's?

- Children experience many different feelings during divorce: anger, hurt, sadness, emptiness, loneliness, relief, guilt, fear, confusion, rage, disappointment, grief, etc.

- Children may not have the vocabulary they need to talk about their feelings. One way to discuss feelings is to ask them to give names of colors or shapes to their feelings. Or ask where on their body they have "bad" feelings.

- Drawing pictures and playing with clay are just two of many ways for children to work out their angry feelings.

- Acknowledging a child's feelings without passing judgement ("I see you are upset" instead of "Don't be upset, silly") or making light of their feelings ("I know that this is hard for you" instead of "You'll get over it") will help a child accept change.

After a morning bear feast of delicious honeynuts and milk, PaPa Bear takes KoKo to the Busy Bee Bear Care Center before going to work.

"MaMa Bear will pick you up after Bear Care," PaPa tells KoKo as they say good-bye.

Ms. Beartrice, the teacher, greets KoKo with a big smile. "Good morning, KoKo," she says, holding the door open. "Don't you look warm and cozy in that nice jacket? Is it new?"

KoKo doesn't answer. KoKo doesn't feel like smiling or talking to Ms. Beartrice today.

- Letting a child know in advance who will pick him or her up at the end of a day at school or daycare is one of those little details that is very important to a child during divorce.

- Being upset is part of the normal grieving process that children of divorce may experience. Let children know that these feelings are natural and to be expected.

- Your former spouse's good qualities may no longer be available to you, but in all probability they are still available to your child.

- Children who believe that their parents are in charge of making decisions about their lives are less likely to feel responsible for what is happening to their family.

After all the other bear cubs arrive, Ms. Beartrice tells them, "Today, we're going to draw pictures of our families. Everyone can get paper and crayons from the shelf."

KoKo takes some drawing paper and crayons and goes to sit next to Patsy Panda. Patsy is KoKo's favorite friend at Bear Care. Patsy is very good at drawing pictures.

The picture Patsy draws has her mother and her father and Patsy in it—everyone in her family.

KoKo takes the crayon and starts to draw a picture of a house. KoKo thinks for a minute. KoKo doesn't know where to put MaMa Bear or PaPa Bear—or even where to put KoKo—in the picture.

KoKo doesn't finish the picture.

- Children, like many parents, often think that only traditional families—two parents and their children—are "normal." In reality, there are many types of "normal" families.

- Children need the chance to ask questions and talk about their feelings but they may not always be ready to talk about them when you are. Give them many opportunities for talks with you.

- Even though children may know others whose parents are divorced, when it happens to them they might feel embarrassed and not want to talk about it to others.

- Stress at home often affects childrens' ability to concentrate in school. During a divorce it is common for children to daydream, be inattentive and have trouble completing assignments.

When the day at Bear Care is over, MaMa Bear comes to pick up KoKo. "Before we go home," says MaMa, "I think we should talk to Ms. Beartrice. We need to tell her about the divorce and the changes at our house."

"Ms. Beartrice," says KoKo, "my daddy doesn't live with us any more."

"That must be hard for you, KoKo. Is that why you did not finish your picture of your family?" she asks.

"I didn't know where to put any of us," says KoKo.

"KoKo, your mother and I want to talk for a minute. Why don't you go and say good-bye to Patsy," says Ms. Beartrice. "By the way, KoKo, did you know that Patsy Panda's parents are divorced, too?"

Koko remembers that Patsy's picture had her whole family in it.

- Telling family, friends, teachers and caregivers about your divorce is not easy but it is important to do so in a timely fashion. How you do this sets an example for your child.

- Sometimes children are embarrassed or angry when teachers are informed about their family's divorce. This is normal so don't let yourself be annoyed with such behavior and don't allow a child's sensitivity stop you from notifying the school.

- Children do not need to be privy to all discussions between parents especially those regarding financial matters.

- Even though divorce is no longer uncommon in our society, children still feel unique when it happens to them.

- Teachers will assume children live with both parents unless they are told otherwise.

When they are in the car MaMa Bear asks, "Where's your bearpack, KoKo?"

"Oh no, I left it at PaPa Bear's house," KoKo remembers. "I'm sorry. I forgot it. I didn't mean to."

"Don't worry, KoKo. I understand that having two homes makes remembering everything harder," says MaMa Bear. "We'll just drive by and pick it up or ask PaPa Bear to bring it over later.

"One more thing, KoKo. Remember that no matter where we live or who we live with, we are all still your family. PaPa and I are divorcing each other but we are not divorcing you. A divorced family is still a family."

KoKo is not so sure. This divorced family doesn't feel like the family KoKo remembers—or wants.

- Shared parenting will have glitches. Don't let that be your excuse for thinking it isn't working. Time smooths out most problems, but shared parenting—like life—is never perfect.

- If possible, avoid last-minute surprises or changes in plans involving your children. Impromptu changes can create anger, disappointment and loss of trust in your child as well as in the other parent.

- It is normal for young children to be careless about their possessions. Weekly checklists can be helpful for parents and children alike.

- Keep in mind that every problem or difficulty your child has is not necessarily related to your divorce.

- Parents who act like parenting partners when divorcing help their children feel more secure. And that, after all, is the job of a parent.

That evening when MaMa and KoKo are making dinner, KoKo tells MaMa Bear, "I don't like this divorce. Sometimes it makes me mad and sometimes it makes me sad."

"I know this is not easy for you, but with time I think you will feel better," says MaMa Bear.

Then MaMa Bear has an idea. "KoKo," she says, "let's pick a day on next month's calendar and we'll see what your feelings are like on that day. We'll call it a *Feelings-Check Day*. If your sad or mad feelings are not gone on that day, we'll pick another day the next month and check again. I'm sure that on one of the days we choose you will be able to say your feelings are not so very sad or mad anymore."

KoKo likes that idea. Since Sunday is KoKo's favorite day, they draw a big red check on the middle Sunday of next month's calendar.

- Creating a color-coded calendar can help parents and children keep track of which days children are at which parent's home.

- It is good to send some of your child's school work along with your child when time with the other parent is only on weekends. Children want to share their efforts and accomplishments with both of their parents.

- Children need to know that life will get better with time and that they won't always feel as they do now. (Things do not always get better for children whose parents continue to fight furiously.)

- Ask children for input when you're not sure how to handle a situation. You don't have to act on their suggestions but it may provide some insights. But don't ask, "Who do you want to live with?"

After dinner MaMa and KoKo work on a puzzle.

"Families are a lot like a puzzle, KoKo," says MaMa Bear. "Each of us is like one puzzle piece. When PaPa and I got married we fit together just right. We loved each other and were so happy when you were born. But things changed and now PaPa and I don't fit together anymore."

"You know that when a puzzle piece doesn't fit, all the pushing in the world doesn't make it fit. In fact, pushing too hard can break that piece. The good news, KoKo," continues MaMa Bear, "is that parents are *always* the right fit with their children even when the parents don't fit together anymore."

"Maybe that's true, but I still wish we could be just one puzzle all together," says KoKo.

"I know, KoKo, I know," says MaMa Bear. "Divorce is not easy."

- Looking through your child's baby photos together is a chance to talk about how much your child was wanted and enjoyed when he or she was born.

- Knowing that parents no longer love each other is painful for a child. But children have the right to love each parent regardless of what has transpired between their parents.

- Never let the other parent's negative attitude or behavior get in the way of letting your children know how much you love them. Be consistent, be there for them and time will work in your favor.

- Avoiding contact with a difficult former spouse—if it also results in not seeing your child—may spare you pain, but not your child.

That night at bedtime MaMa Bear tells KoKo, "You know, nothing you did made us get a divorce. It's not your fault, KoKo Bear, that PaPa Bear and I don't fit together anymore. But you fit me just perrrrrfectly," she says lovingly.

"Now it's time for our bedtime bear blessing:

> *You are the Bear for whom we care.*
>
> *You are so blessed, none can compare."*

KoKo loves it when MaMa says the bedtime blessing.

"Remember, KoKo, PaPa Bear and I each love you so-o-o-o-o-o much and it's okay for you to love each of us even if we're vorced," says MaMa Bear.

- Familiar routines, especially at bedtime, are important in times of change. It will be comforting for your child if bedtime rituals are generally similar in both homes.

- While it may be very hard to give your child permission to love the other parent—especially if you are the one who was "left"—it is important to do so.

- As difficult as it may be for you, try to let your child know that the other parent had many good, decent qualities that you once loved.

- Be sure children know they don't have to choose between parents and that both parents will always love them.

Another night at bedtime at PaPa Bear's house, PaPa tells KoKo, "You know, nothing you did made us get a divorce. It's not your fault that MaMa Bear and I don't fit together anymore. But you fit me just perrrrrfectly," he says lovingly.

"Now it's time for our bedtime bear blessing:

You are the Bear for whom we care.

You are so blessed, none can compare."

KoKo loves it when PaPa says the bedtime blessing.

"Remember, KoKo, MaMa Bear and I each love you so-o-o-o-o-o much and it's okay for you to love each of us even if we're divorced," says PaPa Bear.

- Frequent and consistent parenting arrangements work best for children by giving them a routine they can count on. Similar parenting styles and household rules are helpful but not critical to children's adjustment to separate homes.

- It is normal for children to fantasize for a long time that their parents will reunite. Let your children understand that wishing is okay (they can't help how they feel) but state patiently and lovingly that wishing will not make good things happen (parents getting back together) or bad things happen (wishing someone would die).

- Children need to be able to love and admire both parents. When one parent is constantly put down by the other, regardless of how valid the criticism may be, the child—who is part of the criticized parent—feels put down as well.

The next week as PaPa and KoKo drive over to MaMa Bear's house, KoKo asks, "PaPa, can we be a family even if we don't all live together?"

"Of course we can, KoKo. We are still a family, but now we are a family who lives apart," replies PaPa Bear. "Gramma and Grampa Grizzly don't live with us but they are still part of our family, aren't they, KoKo? And MaMa's sister, Aunt Bearoque and Cousins Beanie and Barney, they don't live with you either, but they are part of our family."

"Yes, you're right. They don't live with us at either house," says KoKo beginning to smile, "and they are still part of my family." KoKo feels better.

KoKo runs to MaMa Bear, gives her a big bear hug and waves good-bye to PaPa Bear. It's still hard to say good-bye to PaPa Bear but it doesn't feel so strange anymore.

- Letting the other parent know how much you appreciate his or her parenting efforts will have a long term payoff for your child. Remember that praise—not criticism—motivates.

- Be careful about sharing your money worries with your child. Children can interpret "We have no money" literally. This is different from saying "We can't afford this right now."

- Children like to take some of their "stuff" with them when they go from home to home. This can be especially irritating when items taken to the other parent's are gifts you've just given. It's normal to feel resentment but resist the temptation to verbalize it—at least not within your children's earshot. It's better to let such items go with them. In this way, a part of you goes with them, as well.

Sometimes KoKo forgets to take the bearpack to PaPa's house and sometimes KoKo leaves a favorite book at MaMa's house. "Everything would be so much easier," thinks KoKo, "if we all lived together." But KoKo also knows that living all together would not be easier for MaMa and PaPa Bear.

KoKo knows that forgetting a book or a bearpack may be KoKo's fault, but MaMa and PaPa's divorce *is not* KoKo Bear's fault.

One day MaMa and KoKo find a *Feelings-Check Day* on the calendar when KoKo's sad and mad feelings are no longer very sad or very mad at all. MaMa Bear was right! On that day MaMa and KoKo draw a big smiley face on the calendar.

Yes, KoKo has two homes and two parents.

Yes, KoKo Bear's parents are divorced but KoKo Bear isn't divorced from anyone. MaMa and PaPa and KoKo Bear are all still a family…just a family apart.

- Building a relationship and a history with each parent is important in the life of a child. The only way to achieve this is to allow children to spend significant time with each parent. Every family's parenting plan needs to be based on this although no two families will ever do it in exactly the same way.

- Parenting plans, like clothes, will be outgrown from year to year and need to be "altered to fit."

- Divorce can be difficult and painful, but divorce in itself doesn't damage children. How you handle your divorce, however, can.

DIVORCE IS A CHALLENGING TIME
Let Vicki Lansky and KoKo Bear Help Your Family

Vicki Lansky's DIVORCE BOOK FOR PARENTS
Helping Your Children Cope With Divorce and Its Aftermath

Sound information dealing with the realities of parenting and divorce: what age-related behavior to expect, learning "divorce-speak," facts about custody, money and legalities, resource references, tips on handling transfer of kids, re-entry behavior, holidays, your dating and much more. Paperback. 240 pages.

IT'S NOT YOUR FAULT, KOKO BEAR,
A Read-Together Book for Parents & Young Children During Divorce

In the unisex character KoKo Bear, children find a friend who learns as they do that they are loved and will be cared for, even though their parents are divorced. The book also contains helpful tips for parents on each page. Hardcover and paperback. 32 pages.

KOKO BEAR

An adorable, soft plush teddy bear to accompany IT'S NOT YOUR FAULT, KOKO BEAR. As lovable as the character in the story, this cuddly bear measures 7" from head to toe and is made of child-safe materials. KoKo Bear comes with a detachable "bear pack" —just the place to hold a child's worries about divorce in the family. KoKo Bear will be a special little friend for those times when a child needs comforting. Perfect for someone who doesn't like this divorce and doesn't want two homes. (Call for price and availability.)

To order single copies of the above titles,
call 1-800-255-3379 or 612-912-0036.

PRACTICAL PARENTING Books-By-Mail
15245 Minnetonka Blvd, Minnetonka MN 55345

A free catalog of all books by Vicki Lansky is available upon request.

Counselors, mediators, lawyers, and divorce support or parent education groups are eligible
for a professional discount when buying 9 or more copies of the above books.
Contact BOOK PEDDLERS at 800-255-3379 for more information.